Moving Day

Amy Houts

Art by Kate Daubrey

Literacy Consultants
David Booth • Kathleen Corrigan

Today is moving day.
Reed and his family are moving.
They are moving
to another town.

They have the boxes.
They have the truck.
They are ready to move!

Sam is Reed's friend.
Sam comes to say good-bye.

Reed is sad.
He will miss Sam.

Reed will miss Grandpa too.

Reed loves Grandpa.

Grandpa lives next door.

"Hi, Reed," says Grandpa.
"You look sad."

"I do not want to move," says Reed.
"I will miss you."

"I know," says Grandpa.
"I was sad when I moved too."

"When did you move?"
asks Reed.

"I moved when I was a boy,"
says Grandpa.
"We moved from far away.
We came here on a ship."

"We are not moving far away,"
says Reed.
"We are going by car."

"I want to show you something,"
says Grandpa.
"Come inside."

Grandpa turns on his computer.

"Look!" says Reed.
"That is a picture of you and me.
I was a baby."

"Here is a picture of me,"
says Grandpa.
"I was a young boy."

"You were a boy too, Grandpa.
You had to move,"
says Reed.

"Yes," says Grandpa.
"I was brave.
You will be brave too."

"Can I have this picture?"
asks Reed.
"It will make me feel brave."

"Yes," says Grandpa.

"Here it is," says Grandpa.

"Thank you," says Reed.

"Bye, Grandpa," says Reed.

"I will see you soon," says Grandpa.

Reed gets into the car.
He is brave now.